YOUR PERFECT WEDDING VOWS

A GUIDE TO ROMANTIC AND LOVING WORDS FOR YOUR CEREMONY

BY LAURIE SUE BROCKWAY

This book is dedicated to all the couples making their way to the altar and looking for the right words to express their love and share what is in their hearts.

I hope you come away from this book realizing that your vows can be anything you want them to be, and as personal and romantic as you wish.

*Enjoy the journey of writing, selecting, or adapting **Your Perfect Wedding Vows.***

Your Perfect Wedding Vows
Copyright © 2015 by Laurie Sue Brockway

Cover Design by Niina Cord
Copy editing by Wendy Schuman
Published by Wedding Goddess Communications

ISBN-13: 978-1-941630-01-3

Standing at the Altar of Love

Here we stand before those we love,
Pledging ourselves to one another,
For all time.

We come here of our own free will,
Having chosen one another,
And knowing that marriage is a big step.

We come here in the spirit of love,
Filled with hope for our future,
And confident that our love can see us through challenges.

We come here not knowing exactly what life will bring,
But knowing we want to experience it together,
And trusting our commitment is strong enough to last forever.

On this day, as we pledge our love and devotion,

May our bond be strengthened.
May our hearts and souls be joined.
May we grow in love and respect for one another.
May we grow in our devotion to one another.
May our marriage always be our home.

-Laurie Sue Brockway

TABLE OF CONTENTS

INTRODUCTION

So Many Unique Couples, So Many Romantic Vows

"The exchange of vows is the heart of the wedding ceremony."
-Peg Kehret, from Wedding Vows

Your wedding vows are often considered the hallmark of the wedding ceremony. They are meant to acknowledge your love and commitment, to share what you mean to each other, and to express promises that will build the foundation of your marriage. Personal vows are not a "legal" part of your ceremony, so they can be highly unique and romantic!

In my experience as a wedding officiant, I have discovered many different ways couples can express their love in wedding vows, and wedding words, that are meaningful. Sometimes this takes the form of vows they write themselves, sometimes they borrow from favorite readings or songs, and sometimes they opt for classic or traditional vows that are romantic and have endured through time.

This book contains many different ways to include personal and personalized wedding vows in your ceremony. Some are classic, and many are unique. The second part of this book has an array of sample vows. Please feel free to adapt them, or be inspired by them, when creating your own vows. Most of the samples were used with the permission of many of the happy couples I have had the honor to work with in my wedding ministry. My belief is that you and your beloved should have input and approval over what you decide to share and how you decide to share it.

The third part of this book discusses ways to include other written documents in your ceremony, such as love letters, and intentions for married life.

The final part of this book offers tips on how to keep your wedding vows alive in your relationships and make the romance last beyond the wedding by repeating your vows privately to one another and writing new ones as the years go by.

Here are some simple tips for writing your wedding vows:

Words and promises of love, adoration, and commitment are an important part of your ceremony. Use them thoughtfully.

- Choose language and sentiments that are truly meaningful.
- Pay tribute to each other and the relationship you have built together.
- Find a way to express your vows that allows you both to truly look forward to making your promises to love, honor, cherish, and more.
- Never force the writing of your vows or push yourself to speak vows when it doesn't feel right.
- Trust that the wedding altar is a safe place for you both to share what is in your hearts. Often, the rest of the world will fade away and it will feel like it is just the two of you there, sharing an intimate, loving, and deeply romantic moment.

PART ONE

Personalizing Your Vows

Personalized vows are a wonderful way to express your love on your wedding day. Although your whole ceremony can be an expression of love and commitment, the promises you make to one another are the hallmark of your sacred ceremony.

Public speaking may not be your thing, so it is important that you do not stress yourself over vows. But it is so helpful, together with your beloved, to give the vows some thought and be willing to speak them from the heart and soul. Contained within those words are the seeds of dreams to come, intentions for your marriage, and deep declarations of love.

CHAPTER ONE

Decide What Type of Wedding Vows Are Right for You

While you may have a certain reference or preconceived notion of what a wedding vow is meant to be, there are many different options for expressing your love and commitment in the form of vows, promises, and stories. You and your beloved should pick an option most suited to the two of you, taking into consideration the following:

- Is it important for you to write your own personal vows in your own unique voice?
- Would you consider adapting your vows from a vow book or from vows written by other couples?
- How comfortable are you both about speaking in front of friends and family?
- Would it be less stressful for you to write or select vows you like, but have your officiant present them in the ceremony as questions you "agree" to rather than promises you speak out loud?
- Do you imagine yourself reading vows to each other, or would you prefer to have your officiant guide you through the vows in repeat-after-me fashion?

Where Do Religion and Culture Fit In?

Traditional and classic vows, as well as familiar religious vows, can also be very romantic and meaningful, or can be adapted in a way to make them more personal.

Think about whether you would like to include religious, cultural references, or even pop culture in your vows.

Unless you are to be married in a religious ceremony that will follow a time-honored religious protocol, you can be as creative as you like. The range of options is vast.

Your vows may depend on the kind of ceremony you are having and the romantic and loving sentiments already expressed in the blessings, prayers, readings, and cultural or religious aspects of the service. For example, if you are having an interfaith wedding that is bringing in Christian and Hindu elements, you may opt for classic Christian vows blended with classic Hindu vows.

Alternatively, you might consider traditional and classic elements of your faiths and cultures, and then look for ways to blend traditions you like with creativity, romance, and personal touches.

This could mean sharing a humorous story of how you met. For example, a couple I married had a Christian and Interfaith service, but in the minister's message, which is more informal, I shared the story of how they met in a New York bar during a raging snowstorm. In their vows, they each included references to that fateful night. Or you might include a poignant poem that captures your feelings and can be used instead of writing something on your own. One groom read the full version of "The Invitation," by Oriah Mountain Dreamer (a poem he and his fiancée loved) and it was spectacular.

Identify the Overall Vibe for Your Wedding

As a reference point, here are several types of wedding ceremonies. If you think about which best defines the kind of ceremony you are having, it may help you more clearly define the kinds of vows you would like.

Traditional. These are typically faith-based and culled from the tradition into which the bride and groom were born.

Non-denominational. A spiritual ceremony that includes reference to God, but does not adhere to any particular religious protocol.

Non-religious. Usually includes no reference to faith and typically does not mention God.

Interfaith. When the couple come from different faith traditions, this kind of ceremony combines the two by including aspects of religion or religious rituals or readings that are symbolic of each faith.

Intercultural. This ceremony is a blending of cultures —such as a Filipino veil ceremony with a Chinese red string ritual —and yet can certainly also incorporate religious aspects.

Pop culture theme. This is usually a ceremony adapted from something that is part of popular culture and close to the hearts of the bride and groom. These may range from a medieval-style ceremony in which the couple dress as a knight and lady of the court, to a ceremony including lines from "Star Wars" or Disney, to nuptials based on a favorite romance novel, movie, or even opera.

CHAPTER TWO

'Question of Intent' Vows

In every ceremony there is a question put forth by your officiant that gives you an opportunity to declare that you freely chose to marry the person standing beside you. It's called the "question of intent." Sometimes it is the simple question "Do you come here of your own free will?" More often is the question that brings you to the classic answer: "I do." The intent question is the part of the ceremony that satisfies a legal requirement that the couple declare they are entering into marriage by choice.

If you two feel you do not want to say much during the ceremony, either because you are shy or because the thought of speaking at length makes you too nervous (or terrified), you can have an extended "question of intent" that satisfies the legal requirement (such as, "Do you Colleen take Art to be your husband") and gives you a chance to agree to certain declarations in response to your officiant.

While the intent question is not a wedding vow per se, it can be personalized to incorporate the words and meanings you might choose for your vows. You do not actually have to speak the vows. The officiant asks the question. All you have to do is answer "yes" or "I will."

For example, a traditional intent question many people are familiar with is:

> **Do you Colleen take Art to be your husband,**
> **To have and to hold from this day forward?**
> **In sickness and in health?**
> **In good times and bad times?**
> **Will you love, honor and cherish him,**
> **All the days of your life?**

Here's a more modern approach to the same kind of vow format.

> **Do you, Jane, take Adam, to be your husband?**
> **Do you promise to grow with him in mind and spirit …**
> **To always be open and honest with him …**
> **And cherish him for all the days of your life?**

And here's a way to get a lot of sentiments across without having to speak them.

> **Do you Alice take Jonathan**
> **to be your lawfully wedded husband from this day forward?**
> **In the presence of God, family, and friends,**
> **Do you offer him your solemn vow …**
> **to be his faithful partner**
> **in sickness and in health,**
> **in good times and in bad,**
> **and in joy as well as in sorrow?**
> **Do you promise to love him unconditionally,**
> **Support him in his goals,**

Honor and respect him,
Laugh with him and cry with him,
and to cherish him
for as long as you both shall live?

To all of these you will, of course, answer "I do."

CHAPTER THREE

'Repeat After the Officiant' Vows

You might also wish to have a set of vows spoken individually *in addition to* the question of intent (either right after or before) or as part of your ring vows (during the blessing and exchange of rings). These vows should be of a manageable length and can be "fed" to each of you in bite-size pieces by your officiant so that you don't have to memorize anything and can repeat them easily. Any of these vows can be adapted for husband and wife, husband and husband, or wife and wife.

Here's an example from Sophia and Zvonko's ceremony:

1. Basic Vow Outline Repeated by Each Partner:

**I, Sophia [or Zvonko], promise
To trust and respect you ...
Be patient and understanding...
Openly share my thoughts,
And share my fears and dreams ...
Watch after your well-being ...
Nurture your growth ...
And bring lightness and joy to our lives.
I will be a loving and supportive partner.**

2. A Classic Vow Revised to Include Modern Sentiments:

You can also take a classic vow and mix it up with romantic and meaningful promises that are important to you both. You each speak the entire vow, repeating after the officiant. For example:

I, Carol, take you, Jason,
to be my lawfully wedded husband from this day forward.
In the presence of God, our family, and friends,
I offer you my solemn vow …
to be your faithful partner
in sickness and in health,
in good times and in bad,
and in joy as well as in sorrow.
I promise to love you unconditionally,
to support you in your goals,
to honor and respect you,
to laugh with you and cry with you,
and to cherish you
for as long as we both shall live.

3. Sharing a Longer Vow.

If you have a vow that is on the long side, instead of having you each repeat the same lines, you can speak part, your beloved can speak part, and then together you can repeat the final lines. This can also be done in repeat-after-the-officiant fashion. Chris and Lori adapted this vow, in part, from Roy Croft's classic poem "Love."

Chris:
Lori, I love you
Not only for what you are,

but for who I am
when I am with you.
Not only for what you have made of yourself…
But for what you are making of me.

Lori:
Kris, I love you…
For helping me to see
the dreams I have for life
more clearly than ever before.
One of those dreams is becoming realized,
right now,
as we come together as a family.

Lori and Kris together:
I promise to you today …
that I will forever fulfill my role …
as your partner …
in the life we are building together.

4. Vows exchanged with rings.

If you prefer to speak your vows along with your rings, which is common in the Christian tradition, you might have a vow like this one that Elizabeth and Ross found in the *The Everything Vows Book.*

Take this ring
As a sign of my love for you
And my commitment to this union.
This is the beginning.
I will be with you until the end.

5. Simultaneous vows.

One way to do something different is to speak the same vow, simultaneously. This is like stereo vows -- you hear it consciously and subconsciously -- and it is really a nice touch to share your sentiments and promises to each other at the same time. It represents partnership and working in the spirit of harmony and cooperation. For example, you might have a vow like this one. I wrote it for a couple who were stressed about writing vows but not about speaking them:

On this day,
a new adventure begins.
I want you to know
That I will stand by your side,
As your partner in life.
I look forward to laughing with you,
Crying with you,
Comforting you,
And being comforted by you,
Inspiring you,
And being inspired by you.
I will always cheer you on
As you follow your dreams.
And I will let you help me achieve mine.
Let us grow together,
In mind and spirit,
And stand together to face the world.
I will cherish you always.
You are my one and only true love.

CHAPTER FOUR

Reading Your Vows to One Another

If you have a lot to share with one another, it may be a little too unwieldy to approach vows in a repeat-after-the-officiant style. And perhaps it is redundant to read the same long vow to one another. Mix it up!

You can always call upon the classic approach of writing or adapting vows you read to each other. Or try a unique approach to reading to one another, using a favorite poem or song. Once in a blue moon a brave soul will memorize or speak from the heart, but unless you are a professional actor or someone who speaks professionally and is completely at ease before an audience, I don't recommend trying to memorize your vows for your wedding day!

Many couples find that reading their own vows is where the tears flow easily—they shy away from it, fearing they will be too nervous. Yet it is often the most authentic and beautiful part of the ceremony. Here are some ideas for highly personalized vows.

1. Writing and reading your own vows. Of course, the time-honored way to share vows is to each write your own separate vows and read them to one another at the wedding altar.

Some couples like to coordinate their vows; others choose to share them for the first time on the wedding day, surprising each other. Either way, it is always a beautiful and touching moment.

Some couples opt for completely unique vows, and others like to add in some traditional sentiments, such as these vows from Katerina and Xingmin (pronounced *Shin-min*).

We printed their vows on beautiful scroll paper for an elegant touch.

Katrina:

Xingmin, I love you for being gentle, kind, and tender.
I love you for hearing my thoughts, sharing my dreams.
I love you for filling my life with joy and loving me without end.
I love you for accepting me as I am.
With you, I can be completely happy and completely myself.
From this day, I promise to love, honor, and cherish you, in sickness and health, in good times and bad.
I pledge myself to be ever faithful to you, with my body, my mind and my heart.
I freely take you as my husband.

Xingmin:

Kaca (her nickname), I consider my decision to learn ballroom dancing the best decision I ever made in my life. That's how I met you, got to know you, and fell in love with you.
I love you because you are beautiful, intelligent, and kind.
I love you because you make me happy and you make me whole.

From this day, I promise to love, honor, and cherish you, in sickness and health, in good times and bad.
I pledge myself to be ever faithful to you, with my body, my mind, and my heart.
I freely take you as my wife.

2. Alternating line vows: You can also decide to divvy up the lines and alternate reading to one another. This is a very creative and somewhat theatrical way to share your vows. It's very special. Here are the vows Tony and Summer wrote and read to each other. We made it easier to follow by printing the bride and groom's lines in different colors (their favorite wedding colors of course!).

Summer: **My darling Tony, you are the magic of my days.**

Tony: **My darling Summer, you help me to laugh and teach me to love.**

Summer: **This I promise to you:**
I will always be honest, kind, patient, and forgiving.

Tony: **This I promise to you: I will encourage your individuality because that is what makes you unique and wonderful.**

Summer: **I will nurture your dreams, because through them your soul shines.**

Tony: **I will help shoulder our challenges, because through them we'll emerge stronger.**

Summer: I will share with you the joys of life, because with you they will be that much sweeter.

Tony: I will be your partner in all things, working with you as a part of the whole.

Summer: I will be a true and loyal friend to you.

Tony: I will cherish you, hold you, and honor you.

Summer: I will respect you, encourage you, and cherish you, in health and sickness.

Both: Through sorrow and success, for all the days of my life.
I will love you with all of my heart.
These are my sacred vows to you, my equal in all things.

3. Other ideas for vows: Be as creative as you would like! If you would rather select or adapt vows from poetry or a song, go for it. For example:

- Tim and Patty adapted two of their favorite songs for the ceremony. Tim read the lines from Chicago's "Inspiration," and Patty shared sentiments found in "From This Moment" by Shania Twain. Then she had a guitarist and singer play it live immediately after she and Tim exchanged vows.

- Maria and Michael used poetry. The bride was shy about speaking, so Michael read Oriah Mountain Dreamer's stirring poem, "The Invitation."

- Steven and Deborah chose not to speak vows themselves and instead had their officiant *read* their favorite song, "My First, My Last, My Everything" by Barry White.

4. Speaking from the heart—without a script. Some brides and/ or grooms prefer to speak without a piece of paper. As mentioned, I don't recommend that you try to memorize your vows. It may be too stressful on your wedding day, and your brain often goes into an altered state. Yet by all means if you or your beloved prefer to simply "share" what is in your hearts, do so.

At the Central Park wedding of Kelly and Ron, the groom launched into a personal declaration of his love that had us all in tears and elicited cheering and clapping from some 200 onlookers who had quietly gathered to watch the intimate ceremony. It was a totally natural and spontaneous expression of his love. Another couple, Jodelle and Juan, had written and prepared their own vows, but one second in, the groom declared he was not one to follow a script and proceeded to tell his beloved how much she meant to him. It was amazing and so touching. And it worked for them.

If one of you needs to have a piece of paper at the altar — or a card with your vows on it —and the other feels more comfortable just speaking freely, that's fine too.

As the officiant, I also like to keep any written vows close by just in case! One groom I worked with insisted he was going to memorize his vows and that he did not need to have them written down. I had a feeling that he could not know in advance the sometimes overwhelming emotions that can arise while expressing such deep love and affection. My instincts told me to get him to write the vows down. He showed up at the ceremony with vows scribbled on a napkin, and I kept them close. He was very happy when I slid them over to him just as some of what he wanted to say was escaping his memory.

It all worked out fine—it always does—but it strengthened my resolve that it helps to have a back-up of everything you want to say, on paper—even if you never use it. You should be free to approach your vows in any way you want, yet I encourage you not to torture yourself in anyway. And I also encourage you to realize that while you may be the best public speaker in the world, those skills may not all be the present on your wedding day. If you can't bear to read from a piece of paper, honor that impulse—but allow yourself to have at least your talking points nearby.

PART TWO

Ideas to Get You Started on Your Vows

Obviously, there are many ways to celebrate your relationship, promise your love, and affirm your commitment. The most important thing is to make sure your vows are truly meaningful to you both, and that you select a form of communicating your love and intentions for marriage that is comfortable for you both. Below you'll find some techniques that will make it easy for you to create the perfect wedding vows.

CHAPTER FIVE

Vow Writing Exercise

When I first meet with couples about their wedding ceremony, I always give them a writing exercise to help them bring out their feelings of love, friendship, and appreciation. They know they love and adore one another, but they don't always have the language to express it.

The exercise below consists of questions for you and your beloved to think about, together or individually. Take some time to ponder and write down the answers to these questions. Your answers will give you insights on ways to personalize your ceremony, as well as specific ideas and language for the feelings you'd like to express in your vows.

Questions to ponder:
1. How did you meet and what first attracted you to one another?
2. What do you love about each other?
3. What does getting married mean to you?
4. What are some of your dreams and intentions for married life?
5. What story do you want to share about your love?

Chapter Six

Utilizing Other People's Ideas for Your Vows

Borrowing from other sources is completely acceptable in weddings. It could be that the perfect vow already exists out there, and that someone else wrote it as if they were reading your heart and mind. So feel free to consider favorite songs, poems, and other people's vows for ideas. There are many sample weddings and vows posted on the Internet, on sites such as theknot.com. Here are some terrific books on vows, or which include vows:

- *Words for the Wedding: Perfect Things To Say for a Perfect Wedding Day,* by Wendy Paris and Andrew Chesler (Perigee Books)

- *Weddings From The Heart: Contemporary and Traditional Ceremonies for an Unforgettable Wedding,* by Daphne Rose Kingma, (Conari Press)

- *Wedding Vows: How To Express Your Love In Your Own Words,* by Peg Kehret (Meriwether Publishing Ltd.)

- *Diane Warner's Complete Book of Wedding Vows: Hundreds of Way to Say "I do,"* by Diane Warner (Career Press)

- *The Everything Wedding Vows Book: Anything and Everything You Could Possibly Say at the Altar and Then Some,* by Janet Anastasio and Michelle Bevilacqua (Adams Media Corporation)

CHAPTER SEVEN

Brides Share Inspiration For (and From) Their Wedding Vows

I asked 100 brides to share their experiences in creating their vows, where they found inspiration, and how the vows affected them. Here are some of their responses:

"I think I wrote the perfect vows. I was inspired by a set of inspirational candles given to me by a friend. They read: *Gratitude, Safety, Joy, Faith, Truth, Growth, Healing, Love.* I decided these were the principles I wanted to live by and be part of my marriage so I made sure to include each in my vows. I remember Bob thinking he wanted to add something to them ... and my panic since I thought they were totally perfect. The best could not be improved. But in the sprit of sharing I gave them to him to change as he saw fit -- a test of faith. He finally agreed they *were* perfect!"

-- *Susan who married Bob*

"The part of the ceremony that most strengthened our union was when Ron started to speak from his heart. It wasn't planned, rehearsed or read from a card. It was just from the heart."

- *Kelly, who married Ron*

"I think the most sacred thing that we did as a couple when organizing our wedding was when we wrote our vows."

-- Jodie, who married Andrew

"We used words from our favorite songs to share with each other how we felt. Neither of us knew what the other had selected, so it made the expression of those words even more loving. Doing something personal in your wedding vows does make it extra special."

--Patty, who married Tim

"We adapted existing vows, but we both felt that they expressed what we wanted to promise to each other."

- Laura, who married Erez

"Tony and I wrote rather long vows. Each part of the vow was clear, self-contained, and to the point. In general, I encourage couples to keep their vows short and pithy, going right to the heart of what they want to promise each other. That way, the vows can be something you can tuck into your heart … and pull out in those moments when you need to remember them most."

-- Diane, who married Tony

PART THREE

Sample Wedding Vows

The following vows come from many different sources. These are all real vows used by real couples on their wedding days. I share them here with their permission. They are happy to pass along the blessing!

CHAPTER EIGHT

Examples of Personalized Vows

Pat and Andrea's Vows

Pat: I promise to love you always, without reservation or restraint.

Andrea: I will honor, trust, and respect you, my one and only love, for all of my life.

Pat: I will faithfully support you in all of your hopes and dreams and stand with you through all your challenges.

Andrea: I will be your companion, your lover, your best friend, and your equal as we take this greatest journey of our lives together.

Both: I will without fail
In summer's light
In dark of night
In love
With respect

In joy
With honor
Devote myself
To you, my love.

Ally and Jay's Vows
(Adapted from "Love," by Roy Croft)

Ally: I love you for the person you are and for who I have become since we've met.

Jay: I love you for overlooking my flaws and weaknesses and for drawing out the good things in me.

Ally: I love you for believing in me in a way that makes me believe, too.

Jay: I love you because of the way we can talk together and with that comes openness and closeness.

Ally: I love you because you are honest with me and with that honesty comes trust.

Jay: I love you because you have brought more happiness into my life than I ever thought possible.

Ally & Jay: You have done it without a touch, without a word, without a sign. You have done it by being yourself. Perhaps that is what being a friend means, after all.

Jason and Denise's vows

Jason and Denise speak simultaneously:
I ask for nothing more
from this good life
than that I may spend it with you.

I offer my hand and my heart,
and trust utterly
they will be safe with you.

Today, standing here
before God, family, friends
and the city we both love,
I join my life with yours.

Tina and Lawrence's vows

Tina and Lawrence speak simultaneously:
On this day,
our new adventure begins.
I promise
I will stand by your side,
As your partner in life.

I look forward to sharing
Laugher and tears,
Comfort and challenges,
Great joy and triumphs.

I want to inspire you,
And be inspired by you
Be your best cheerleader
As you follow your dreams.
And hear your cheering,
As I achieve mine.

Let us grow together,
In heart, mind, and spirit,
And stand together to face the world.
I will cherish you always.
You are my one and only true love.

Antoinette and Taal's vows

Antoinette:
Taal, I join you in this marriage,
hopeful and optimistic
about the life we will continue to share.
(Pause)
You are my partner and best friend.
Today in front of our friends and family,
I promise to continue to respect you
And to love you always.

Taal:
Antoinette, I join you in this marriage,
hopeful and optimistic
about the life we will continue to share.
(Pause)
You are my partner and best friend.

Today in front of our friends and family,
I promise to continue to respect you

Jacki and Brandon's Vows

Brandon:

On top of all the other vows I make to you on our wedding
day, I also vow to always appreciate how lucky I am to have
someone who makes me feel the way you do.
And I vow to continue to make you feel as special as you
make me feel.
Forever and ever.

Jacki:

You are the love of my life.
You have made me a better person.
Our love for one another is reflected in the way I live my life.
I am truly blessed to be a part of your life,
Which as of today becomes OUR life ... together.

Alex and Amy's Vows

My dearest Amy –

I look at you and know how fortunate I am, to be one
you will call husband, to be the one who will stand by
your side, to be the one who will support you, to be
the one that you love.

Staring into your eyes, I see our future and all its
possibilities, a future engulfed in rapture and glee.

Holding your hand I feel all the struggles, all the joys that have led us to this moment of our lives.

Standing here beside you I take the vow, that from the dawn of our unity to the dusk of our lives, together we will weather all the storms that come and go, and relish the sweet tranquility of every sunny day.

My dearest Alex --

You have been my best friend, mentor, playmate, confidant, and my greatest challenge. But most importantly, the love of my life, the one I dream of at night and think about every moment. You make me smile, you make me laugh, you make me feel loved more than words may gather.

I am truly in bliss to be here today, in the presence of our family and friends, to promise to share with you all you have given to me in our 11 years together.

I will honor you and shower you with many warm and fuzzy kisses —cherish, respect, encourage, and love you, in my weakest and strongest, in our lives as one, forever.

Michael and Diana's vows

Diana:

I, Diana, take you, Michael, to be my husband. To have and to hold

from this day forward
In good times and bad times,
In sickness and in health.
To love, honor, and cherish,
All the days of my life.

Michael:

I, Michael, take you, Diana,
to be my wife.
To have and to hold
from this day forward
In good times and bad times,
In sickness and in health.
To love, honor, and cherish,
All the days of my life.

Amy and Luke's vows

Amy:

I bring myself to you this day to share my life with you.
You can trust my love, for it's real.
I promise to be a faithful mate and to share
and support your hopes, dreams and goals.
I vow to be there for you always;
when you fall, I will catch you;
when you cry, I will comfort you;
when you laugh, I will share your joy.
Everything I am and everything I have is yours,
from this moment forth and for eternity.

Luke:

I bring myself to you this day to share my life with you.
You can trust my love, for it's real.
I promise to be a faithful mate and to share
and support your hopes, dreams and goals.
I vow to be there for you always;
when you fall, I will catch you;
when you cry, I will comfort you;
when you laugh, I will share your joy.
Everything I am and everything I have is yours,
from this moment forth and for eternity.

Brad and Karin's Vows

Karin:

Brad, I take you to be my lifetime partner,
secure in the knowledge that you will be
my constant friend, and my one true love.

I promise to encourage and inspire you, to laugh with you,
and to comfort you in times of sorrow and struggle.

I promise to love you in good times and in bad,
when life seems easy and when it seems hard,
when our love is simple, and when it is an effort.

I promise to cherish you, and to always hold you in my
highest regard. These things I give to you today, and all the
days of our life.

Brad:

Karin, We have traveled together
from Barcelona to Budapest
and Thailand to Tuscany

Tahoe to Mexico and places in between.
And the journey we start today,
Is the beginning of more sites unseen.

And all along the way
I promise you this …

I promise you my life
To help navigate a course
That delivers love
From an everlasting source.

I promise you my dreams
To be shared as they come
Not hidden but joined
Together as one.

I promise you truth
When we're rich or poor
Whether it be sweet
Or bitter to the core.

I promise you trust
Because on this we are built
It is the cover of love
An everlasting quilt.

So thank you my love
For taking my hand
To become my wife
In every land.

Chapter Nine

Vows That Tell a Story

Here's a beautiful way Joe and Kate included the story of the night they met into their vows, as well as giving a shout-out to their beloved dog. Kate and Joe met on a warm Manhattan evening when Joe's dog Duke insisted on a second nighttime stroll down familiar city streets, where they ran into Kate for the second time that night!

This is what they read to one another at their wedding:

Joe and Kate

Joe: "I stand here before you today, the most important and significant day of my life so far, because of a single soul, an unlikely soul at that—Duke. Not only is he the reason that you walked up to me the first time, but if it wasn't for his need to go out just two hours later, I would have missed you the second time around. He knew then, as I know now, that you were perfect. Perfect in so many ways. I let you go once, but I will never let you go again. I came to New York City because of my job, but the dreamer in me, no matter how concealed and quiet he might be, would tell you that I came here to meet you, and I cannot deny that. I love that and I love you.

Kate: "For once and for all, you need to know that Duke was not the only reason we met that night. As I walked home and saw your incredible smile for the second time, something in me recognized you. Even though we had never met ... something in my soul let me take the deepest, most peaceful breath of my life because in the middle of millions of people, I had found you....

"That's not to say that everything is always perfect or as storybook as that first night, because to say that would take away from how rich and textured you've made my life.

"I remember one night early on in our relationship, we had an argument about something or other, and I was sure that it would be the end of us. I was so upset, I just sat on the kitchen floor with my head in my hands. But then I looked up and saw you sitting right next to me. Without ego or pride, we sat there on that awful linoleum floor until we figured it all out. That is why I knew I'd marry you and I can promise you, come what may, that I will always sit on the kitchen floor until we figure it out. I love you with a bigger heart than I ever knew I had. You are my peace, my joy, and, thankfully, my family forever."

Here are some other ways couples have told their stories of love, devotion, the strong connection and respect that they share:

Roger and Melissa

Melissa: "When we were first dating, I felt so comfortable and free to be myself. We made a strong connection, quickly. We just 'fit.' I now realize that you were like a part of me that was missing. I fell in love with you because of your sweet, caring, sensitive, goofy, funny self. I fell in love with you because you make me laugh every single day. Ever since I was a little girl, I have imagined the man I would marry. Amazingly, he had brown hair and hazel or green eyes, just like you. Roger, you are like a part of my soul … a part I would never want to live without."

Roger: "I knew from the moment I saw you that you were the one I was going to marry. You are so genuinely caring for people that it immediately made me fall in love with you. Not only are you caring for people that are virtual strangers but you show such caring, love, and devotion to friends and family. We are both unconditionally bound to our families so our relationship is a perfect fit, although I expect it will make holiday choices tough! I am so grateful to you for introducing me to so many new things in life --from food, to the arts, to diversity in cultures. Portuguese Manor is now my favorite restaurant, but maybe I shouldn't be thanking you for all the pounds I have put on since we met!"

Partha and Tracy

Traci: "There are so many things I love about you, that words aren't really enough. I am incredibly blessed to have you in my life. Your outlook and passion for life is something I immediately fell in love with. I've never met a man that has such a heart of gold. You have the innate ability to make me feel like I'm the most special person in the world, every day. You are exceptionally kind, gentle, affectionate, encouraging, charitable, and loyal—not to mention incredibly handsome and vastly intelligent. I admire your brilliance and passion for your career, and you are one of the most generous people I know, next to my father. It's an extraordinary feeling to find someone in life that loves you unconditionally, and you have exuded your unconditional love for me since day one."

Partha: "The things that I love about you are many. Your amazing confidence, your uncanny intelligence, your personality, your passion for everything you do in life, your strong sense of values, and your striking beauty on the outside —which always takes my breath away— but more importantly the beauty that you exude from the inside, which makes me want to believe in the inherently good in the world. Getting married to you will be the start of a wonderful journey filled with love, respect, commitment, passion, laughter and sharing in all of life's experiences...much like the journey we've have been a part of over the last 6 years. You are the one that adds 'any meaning' to all of it for me."

Elizabeth and Nick

Elizabeth: "I love your sense of humor. You can always make me laugh no matter what kind of mood I am in. I love your morals. You are the most trustworthy, honest, and compassionate person I have ever met. I love the fact that you are an awesome chef; that you can find anything in the cupboard and refrigerator and make a gourmet dinner! I love your eyes, smile, and legs (you have really great legs!). I love that you think the world of me and that even though we disagree on things, you still have utmost respect for my beliefs. I love your 4 AM kisses before heading off to work. I love how you take care of me. You truly are the most amazing man I have ever met. And I am a very lucky woman."

Nick: " I love you for your love of life and dedication to the humane treatment, safety, and health of animals, especially cats. I love you for the way you keep me grounded and focused. I love you because more often than not, you smile, and when you do, it warms my heart and reminds me of how beautiful you are, inside and out."

Chapter Ten

Generic Vows You Can Personalize

I've cobbled together these generic vows to give you some ideas or lines for your own expressions of love. You can use some of the sentiments in these vows to craft a more personalized vow, adding in what you love about each other and what marriage means to you.

This Marriage Is Our Home

Let this marriage be our new home.
May it be warm, loving, and inviting.

Let us embrace those we care about most.
May they join us in a circle of happiness.

Let us build a life and a family here.
May we welcome children and grandchildren.

Let us bless the world with our love,
For surely we have enough to go around.

Here Is My Commitment to You:

I will be there for you
Through all seasons.
And through all life brings our way

In good times and bad,
In sickness and in health,
In happiness and sadness,
In success and disappointment,
In passion and despair,
In celebration and time of change,
And even in those times
when you don't feel like being there,
I will stay there, with you.

Marriage has its ups and downs.
But we will learn to ride the waves together
And we will deal with the tides of change
Together.

I love you and want nothing more in the world than to
be your partner, lover, friend, and for you to call me your
husband/wife.

What Marriage Means

Take my hand,
And walk with me into our new life,
You and me, together,
Blending our lives.

Building our dreams,
Enhancing our passion,
Exploring the world,
Improving ourselves,
Preparing for a family,
Embracing the ones we care for,
Sharing our love,
Leaving our mark,
Creating our legacy of love.
Marriage means we will grow,
and grow older, together.
We will support each other,
And be there for each other,
Through the good,
and not so great times.
We are a pair for life now
And we are meant to stick together,
No matter what,
You and me,
Together,
Holding on to each other,
I want nothing more than to be your husband/wife.

My Beloved Soulmate

I always knew you existed.
But worried that I would never find you.
You are the one I have longed for.
The true love I prayed for.
The partner I envisioned.
The playmate I hoped for.

The best friend I needed.
The wise counsel I sought.
The dear one I wanted to hold near.
With you in it, my life is richer.
On this special day, we pledge our love
And we embark on a special journey together.
We will see the world,
And we will be the world,
For one another.
And so the journey begins.
Thank you for loving me.

Note: Don't forget, you can also use humor and add in cute things about each other in your vows.

Chapter Eleven

Ring Vows

Ring vows are vows that can be spoken during the exchange of rings instead of, or in addition to, personal vows.

Many couples enjoy using short, classic ring vows, or some variation of them. These include:

- **With this ring, I thee wed.**
- **With this ring, I pledge my love.**

Some couples choose a more modern version:

- **With this ring, I marry my best friend.**
- **With this ring, I promise my love and devotion.**

And other couples like to personalize the ring vow to include statements that have a deeper meaning. In any case, your officiant usually leads you through this part of the ceremony.

Here is an example from the wedding of Dawn and Aydin:

Aydin, please take Dawn's hand. Slip the ring on her finger.

> **I give you this ring**
> **as a symbol**
> **of my love for you.**
> **As this ring surrounds your finger,**
> **so my love protects**
> **and surrounds you,**
> **forever and always.**
> **With this ring,**
> **I thee wed.**

Dawn, please take Aydin's hand, slip the ring on his finger.

> **I give you this ring**
> **as a symbol**
> **of my love for you.**
> **As this ring surrounds your finger**
> **so my love protects**
> **and surrounds you,**
> **forever and always.**
> **With this ring,**
> **I thee wed.**

CHAPTER TWELVE

Expression of Intent--Options for 'I Do's'

The expression of intent is a question asked by your officiant and is traditionally answered with "I do." You can have a very basic intent question, such as: "Do you Alix take Jason to be your husband." Or you can go with a more "classic" or personalized question of intent.

Here are some samples:

1. Classic

Do you, Suzan, take Jake, to be your husband?
To have and to hold from this day forward,
In good times and bad times,
In sickness and in health,
To love, honor, and treasure?

Suzan answers: *I DO*

And do you, Jake, take Suzan, to be your wife?
To have and to hold from this day forward,
In good times and bad times,

In sickness and in health,
To love, honor, and treasure?

Jake answers: *I DO*

2. Non-Traditional

Do you, Amy, take Luke, to be your husband?
Do you promise to grow with him in mind and spirit … To always be open and honest with him … And cherish him for all the days of your life?

Amy answers: *I DO*

And do you, Luke, take Amy, to be your wife?
Do you promise to grow with her in mind and spirit… To always be open and honest with her… And cherish her for all the days of your life?

Luke answers: *I DO*

3. Longer Question (gives you a chance to put what you might say in a vow into the "I do" so that you do not have to do much talking):

Do you, Sandy, take Joe to be your husband?
Do you promise to be a faithful mate?
To share your hopes, dreams, and goals?
Will you catch him if he falls? Comfort him when he cries?
Laugh with him in times of joy, and support him in times of challenge?

Today in front of your friends and family,
Do you promise to continue to love and respect him for the rest of your life?

Sandy answers: *I DO*

Do you, Joe, take Sandy to be your wife?
Do you promise to be a faithful mate?
To share your hopes, dreams and goals?
Will you catch her if she falls? Comfort her when she cries?
Laugh with her in times of joy, and Support her in times of challenge?
Today in front of your friends and family,
Do you promise to continue to love and respect her ... for the rest of your life?

Joe answers: *I DO*

PART FOUR

Adding a Little Extra to Your Vows

Your vows are a traditional and classic way to mark the day you say "I do." Yet there are many other ways the written word can help you celebrate the emotional and spiritual bond of your union, as well map your responsibilities --and dreams --as marriage partners.

Knowing that all new marriages can use an extra boost, I like the idea of also having a spiritual or personal love contract.

Chapter Thirteen

Love Contracts That Seal Your Vows

In Judaism the contract between husband and wife is called a Ketubah. Quakers have a spiritual document that the whole congregation signs to bless the union of two people who choose to unite as one. Whether you include a document from your religion or culture, or creatively fashion your own, it will be a blessing on your marriage: a blessing that begins when you and your beloved sit down and write your own personal love contract, marriage agreement, or outline of your intentions for married life. Most often, your agreement will be just between the two of you, not shared with the congregation at your wedding.

Creating a personal love and marriage contract is a beautiful way to clarify what you both anticipate, and what you would like to experience and create in your marriage. It can include everything from being kind and thoughtful every day, to having children, to building a dream house and growing old together. This is not a prenuptial agreement or a legally binding document; rather, it is a spiritually binding document. Here are a few ideas to get you started.

1. Create a Mission Statement for Your Marriage.

The first step of any new enterprise is to create a mission

statement. This applies to your marriage too! Brainstorm, discuss, process, and bat around ideas until you come up with a "Marriage Mission Statement." This is your mutual intention for marriage; it is what you want to be and build together. It can have one sentence or reflect a number of ideas. For example:

Our union is the foundation of our lives. It gives us strength, power, and fortitude to deal with all of life's ups and downs, and it empowers us to contribute to others and the world. We are best friends, confidantes, and partners, and we have many close relationships with people we consider spiritual family. We inspire others and model what it is to be in a great relationship.

2. Craft a Wedding Scroll.

Together, make a list of your intentions, aspirations, goals, hopes, and dreams for your wedded life. Write neatly or type it. It can be on pretty parchment-like paper, or any attractive paper. Consider having it written in calligraphy and framed, or simply roll it up and tie it with a gold ribbon. No one need see it but you two. Take it to your ceremony and keep it at the altar so it will be blessed by the expressions of love and commitment shared at your ceremony, and energized by the vows you exchange. It can include things you thought were too personal to share in front of others. These are very personal statements the two of you can come up with together. For example:

- *We treat our love and our relationship as sacred.*
- *While we include others in our circle of love, we never take our issues outside the relationship, or talk negatively about each other to relatives because this dissipates our sacred bond.*
- *We consult each other on all major life issues, purchases, and plans and yet give one another freedom and space to be individual and do our own thing.*

3. Write Love Letters to Each Other.

Both of you can craft a beautiful letter to each other, stating what you love about each other and what your promises for married life are, and you can place them in a sacred spot in your home, or even include them in the ceremony. My husband, Rev. Vic Fuhrman, MSC, R.M., also an interfaith minister, uses this in ceremonies often and actually hands the letters to the bride and groom and says, "I know you two are utterly in love right now, but take my word for it, there will come a time, be it seven months or seven years from now, when you will have a fight that will make you wonder why you tied the knot in the first place. That's when you will open these letters and remember the spirit of the commitment you made here today."

4. Make a Love Contract.

Type up the wedding vows and declarations from your wedding ceremony, and/or the sentiments shared on your scroll, and add as many more as you feel in your heart. On the bottom of the page, write, "And this I promise to you." Each of you can sign it. Then frame it and keep it next to your bed. Read them over every day, with gratitude.

5. Select a Favorite Poem or Reading.

You can also select something written by another to represent your thoughts, feelings, and intentions for your relationship — a poem, wedding reading, prayer, song or passage from a favorite book. Even a greeting card will do. One couple found a unique sentiment on a card, signed it, and hung it their living room. Although you have to be careful not to step on any copyright laws, it is fine to frame these favorite words and keep them near to inspire you every day.

Chapter Fourteen

How to Keep Your Vows Alive and Well

When you are about to get married, it feels like all the world is filled with love and joy, and nothing can ever happen to shake the strength of your romantic union -- or your faith in the relationship.

During wedding planning, even when there is stress, love feels exciting and new, and it makes couples feel invincible. On the wedding day and honeymoon, you feel enveloped in a bubble of love and enchanted by happiness and sex hormones.

And then... life happens. The bubble can burst.

You may argue, disagree, be exhausted from work or childcare, or experience difficulties and losses that get in the way of your loving feelings and intimate connection.

It's completely normal to begin to lose the "wedding glow" as you set out to build a life together.

In fact, there are those moments in every relationship when two people are so far removed from their wedding day that they more or less forget what brought them together in the first place.

Whether you are an old pro at living together and married life, or just got hitched again for the second time around, over time your marriage needs a tune-up here and there.

Your marriage will hopefully be a long and fruitful journey, but it will need some help along the way.

You can keep your marriage vows alive and keep your relationship fresh by finding ways to renew your commitment to each other every day and to continually acknowledge the sacred promises you made.

It is a good idea to check in every once in a while and make sure you are both still aligned with your wedding vows. In addition, your vows themselves may need some enhancement. As time goes on, you will both change and grow and your married life will evolve.

Even if you did not select or write vows for your wedding, you can select or write "after-wedding vows."

Here are some loving strategies for calling forth those happy feelings again and remembering and honoring the love between you.

1. Sweetly Keeping Your Promises Alive.

We are all pretty high on love and life after the wedding -- that's why they call it the honeymoon period! Anniversaries can also stimulate a lot of those love hormones -- even if you don't think you have any hormones left! They are a good time to reignite the kind of love. Remembering the promises made at the altar can help you both maintain the happy feelings of your very special day. I learned this from one of my deans in seminary school, Rev. Diane Berke, who married for the second time and repeated her wedding vows with her new husband on her honeymoon. They enjoyed it so much they kept going for two years! Why not try it for two weeks or a month? Find your wedding vows or write new ones. Starting on your anniversary or some special occasion, each night before you go to bed, take some time to look deeply into each other's eyes and repeat them to one another.

2. Surround yourself with reminders of your wedding day.

Have you packed up the wedding photos? Bring them out again. And get some beautiful paper, print your vows out and frame them. Keep them in your boudoir, next to your favorite wedding photo, and any other mementos from your wedding that fill your senses with happy memories.

3. Expand your vows.

The vows you speak at your wedding may be on the short side, or tend to be romantic. There may have been some things you felt were too personal, or too practical to add in. And once you have a little experience with marriage under your belt (or a lot!), you may find there are additional sentiments you would like to add to your vows. These are very personal statements the two of you can come up with together. You can add them to your existing vows and repeat them to each other, and frame them, or just keep them in a sacred place -- such as a holy book or even in a frame behind your wedding photo, symbolically making them the foundation beneath your marriage. Over time you can add in anything that you desire as you learn more about what you both hold dear in married life. (See Chapter 12 for some ideas!)

4. Regularly recommit to your marriage. Remember, you can celebrate and recommit to your marriage at any time. Your legal marriage is a one-time deal, yet there is no law that says you cannot renew your commitment at any stage. Consider a re-commitment ceremony every few years. Every time you experience a ritual that declares your love, it's like giving your love, your life, and your marriage a new infusion of energy or even a fresh start.

Parting Blessing

May your wedding vows be a unique and
authentic expression of your love, your commitment,
and the life you choose to live together!

And in your life as married couple, our wish for you is that you
enjoy the life you share to the fullest!

And that you continue to keep falling in love... with each
other... over and over again.

Have a great wedding!

Warmly, Rev. Laurie Sue

This Concludes
YOUR PERFECT WEDDING VOWS
By Rev. Laurie Sue Brockway

WEDDING VOW
BIBLIOGRAPHY

The vows in this book were shared by couples I married. I do not know if they were influenced by a particular book. But here are some of the books I have recommended to my couples, and which I recommend to you, for inspiration.

Anastasio, Janet, Michelle Bevilacqua, Leah Furman, and Elina Furman. *The Everything Wedding Vows Book: Anything and Everything You Could Possibly Say at the Altar—and Then Some.* Holbrook, MA: Adams, 2001.

Ford-Grabowsky, Mary, ed. *Sacred Poems and Prayers of Love.* New York: Doubleday, 1998.

Kehret, Peg. *Wedding Vows: How to Express Your Love in Your Own Words.* Colorado Springs, CO: Meriwether, 1989.

Munro, Eleanor. *Wedding Readings: Centuries of Writing and Rituals for Love and Marriage.* New York: Viking Books, 1989.

Paris, Wendy, and Andrew Chesler. *Words for the Wedding: Perfect Things to Say for a Perfect Wedding Day.* New York: Perigee Books, 2001.

Warner, Diane. *Diane Warner's Complete Book of Wedding Vows: Hundreds of Ways to Say "I Do."* Franklin Lakes, NJ: Career Press, 1996.

Weaver, Joanna. *With This Ring: Promises to Keep*. Colorado
    Springs, CO: Waterbrook Press, 1984.

About the Author

Rev. Laurie Sue Brockway is a leading interfaith minister and nondenominational wedding officiant.

She is widely recognized as an expert on interfaith, intercultural, and highly personalized nondenominational weddings and is known for her warm, loving, and creative approach to marrying couples of all backgrounds and faiths. She has a busy wedding ministry based in New York City and is the author of many books, including *Your Interfaith Wedding* and *Wedding Goddess*.

She has guided thousands of couples on their journey to the altar and beyond. She also specializes in helping couples and families manage wedding conflicts and reduce wedding stress.

New York Magazine recognizes her as one of NYC's top interfaith and non-denominational wedding officiants, as does Joan Hamburg in her book, *City Weddings*.

She is frequently called upon as an expert on love, romance, sex, marriage, and weddings and is a columnist for The Huffington Post.

Visit Rev. Laurie Sue at:

www.YourInterfaithWedding.com
www.WeddingGoddess.com

Contact the author at: *RevLaurieSue@WeddingGoddess.com.*

Find her on Facebook: *https://www.facebook.com/pages/
Rev-Laurie-Sue-Brockway/113651855333954*

Follow her on Twitter: *@revlauriesue*

Also by Laurie Sue Brockway

Your Interfaith Wedding
Wedding Goddess
The Goddess Pages
Pet Prayers and Blessings

www.ingramcontent.com/pod-product-compliance
Lightning Source LLC
Chambersburg PA
CBHW071456070426
42452CB00040B/1535